To
Amanda

Ruth Heller
1988

how
to
hide
a
whip·poor·will
& OTHER BIRDS

With special thanks to
Stephen F. Bailey, Ph.D.
Department of Ornithology
California Academy of Sciences

If
you take
a careful look,
you'll see
how
creatures
in this book
are
CAMOUFLAGED
and out
of view—
although
they're
right
in
front
of
you.

RUTH HELLER'S

how to hide a whip·poor·will

& OTHER BIRDS

Reinforced binding

Grosset & Dunlap

Copyright © 1986 by Ruth Heller. Published by Grosset & Dunlap, a member of The Putnam Publishing Group, New York. Printed in Italy. Published simultaneously in Canada. Library of Congress Catalog Card Number: 86-80285 ISBN 0-448-19027-3 A B C D E F G H I J

At
night
the
WHIP-POOR-WILL
is
heard
because
it's
a
nocturnal
bird.

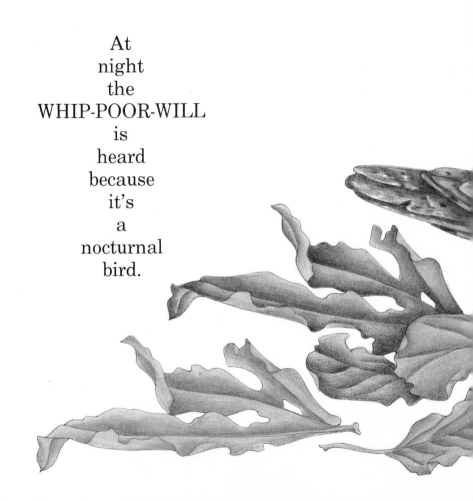

By day it rests
upon the ground
and cannot easily...

be
found.

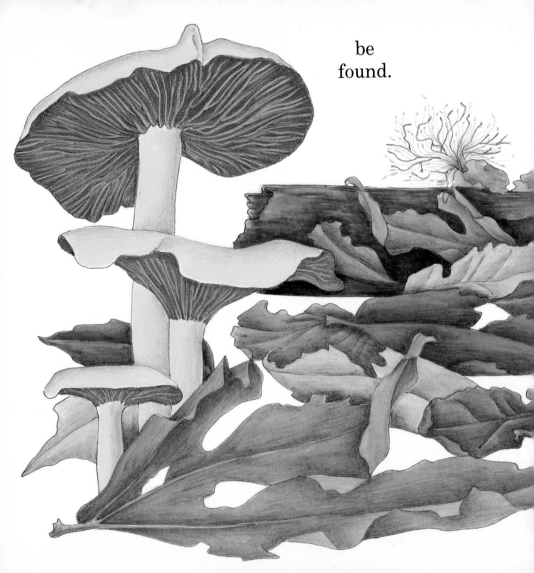

Nocturnal,
too,
is
the
POTOO,
who
in
the
jungle
likes
to
doze
in…

an
upright,
rigid
pose.

At
dawn
the
SCREECH
OWL...

shuts
its
eyes
and
then
is
hard
to
recognize.

In
its
tropical retreat,
this
PLUM-HEADED
PARAKEET...

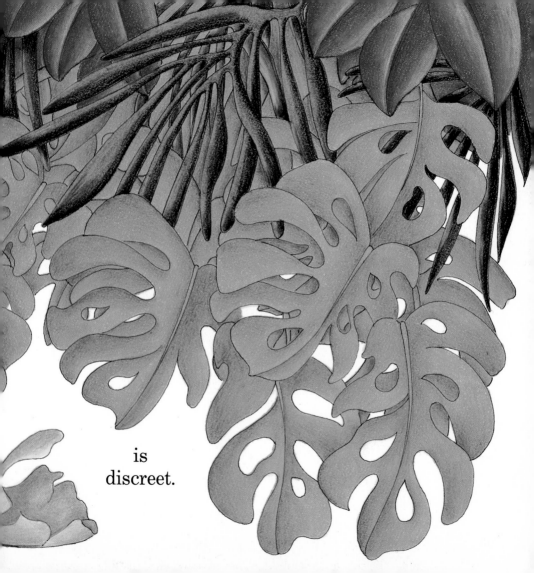

is
discreet.

With
stripes
upon
her
neck and breast,
a
BITTERN,
sitting
on her nest,
sways
with the reeds
as they are
blowing…

so
that
she
is
barely
showing.

When
seen beside her
ornate
mate,
this
WOOD DUCK
may not
look
first-rate,

but
while
all
eyes
are
watching
him…

she is roosting
on
a
limb.

The
PLOVER
doesn't
build
a
nest.

Her
eggs
are
unprotected.
They…

look just like the rocks
nearby and so go
undetected.